Raptor World

Ospreys

by Jenna Lee Gleisner

D1709413

Bullfrog
Books

Ideas for Parents and Teachers

Bullfrog Books let children practice reading informational text at the earliest reading levels. Repetition, familiar words, and photo labels support early readers.

Before Reading

- Discuss the cover photo. What does it tell them?
- Look at the picture glossary together. Read and discuss the words.

Read the Book

- "Walk" through the book and look at the photos. Let the child ask questions. Point out the photo labels.
- Read the book to the child, or have him or her read independently.

After Reading

- Prompt the child to think more. Ask: Ospreys are sometimes mistaken for eagles. Have you seen an eagle or osprey? How are they similar?

Bullfrog Books are published by Jump!
5357 Penn Avenue South
Minneapolis, MN 55419
www.jumplibrary.com

Library of Congress Cataloging-in-Publication Data

Names: Gleisner, Jenna Lee, author.
Title: Ospreys / by Jenna Lee Gleisner.
Description: Bullfrog books edition. Minneapolis, MN : Jump!, Inc., [2020]
Series: Raptor World
Audience: Age 5-8. | Audience: K to Grade 3.
Includes index.
Identifiers: LCCN 2018038751 (print)
LCCN 2018039697 (ebook)
ISBN 9781641286336 (e-book)
ISBN 9781641286329 (hardcover : alk. paper)
ISBN 9781641288231 (pbk.)
Subjects: LCSH: Osprey—Juvenile literature.
Classification: LCC QL696.F36 (ebook)
LCC QL696.F36 G54 2020 (print)
DDC 598.9/3—dc23
LC record available at https://lccn.loc.gov/2018038751

Editor: Susanne Bushman
Designer: Jenna Casura

Photo Credits: Vladimirovic/iStock, cover; NormanBateman/iStock, 1; clsgraphics/iStock, 3; Biosphoto/Superstock, 4; Ilze P/Shutterstock, 5; Ingo Arndt/Minden Pictures/Superstock, 6–7; Nick Garbutt/Superstock, 8–9; Wulong Tommy/Shutterstock, 10–11; Vladimir Kogan Michael/Shutterstock, 12–13; Collins93/Shutterstock, 14, 23tr; Joel Sartore/National Geographic, 15, 23br; FotoRequest/Shutterstock, 16–17; AR Artur Rydzewski/Shutterstock, 18; Kris Wiktor/Shutterstock, 19; BrianEKushner/iStock, 20–21, 23tl; B_Seaman/iStock, 22; Alexander Raths/Shutterstock, 23bl; johnandersonphoto/iStock, 24.

Printed in the United States of America at Corporate Graphics in North Mankato, Minnesota.

Table of Contents

Good Fishers

This nest is big.

nest

It is up high.
How high?
Thirty to 100 feet
(9 to 30 meters) up!

This nest is by water.

Why?

An osprey looks
for fish to eat.

nest

It sees one!

It takes off.

It dives toward
the water.

It stretches out its feet.
See its sharp talons?

talon

The talons dig in.
It catches a fish!

The fish is slippery.
But it cannot escape.

scale

The feet have scales.
They help grip.

The bird carries its prey.

Where?

Back to its nest.

beak

It is time to eat.
The sharp beak helps.

18

It tears off each piece. Yum!

The mom feeds her chicks.

They will grow up.

They will hunt.

chick

21

Built to Hunt

wings
Ospreys have long, narrow wings. They make a crooked M shape when they fly.

beak
The black beak is hooked. This helps the osprey tear and eat its food.

eyes
Adult osprey eyes are yellow. Ospreys have great eyesight and can see fish from great heights.

talons
Large, sharp talons help ospreys grab, carry, and hold onto prey.

Picture Glossary

chicks
Baby ospreys.

grip
To keep a tight hold
on something.

prey
Animals that are hunted
by other animals for food.

scales
Thin, flat, overlapping
pieces of hard skin.

23

Index

To Learn More

Finding more information is as easy as 1, 2, 3.

❶ Go to www.factsurfer.com

❷ Enter "ospreys" into the search box.

❸ Click the "Surf" button to see a list of websites.